Maria Theresa (1717–1780)
Biography of a Monarch

Elfriede Iby

Maria Theresa (1717–1780)
Biography of a Monarch

ISBN 3-901568-57-3
NE: Elfriede Iby

1st edition 2009-09-08

Layout and typesetting: ALPINA Druck, Steinlechner Gabriele
Printed by: ALPINA Druck GmbH/Innsbruck
Translations: Ingrid Haslinger, Sophie Kidd

ISBN 3-901568-57-3

Contents

The Habsburg Empire

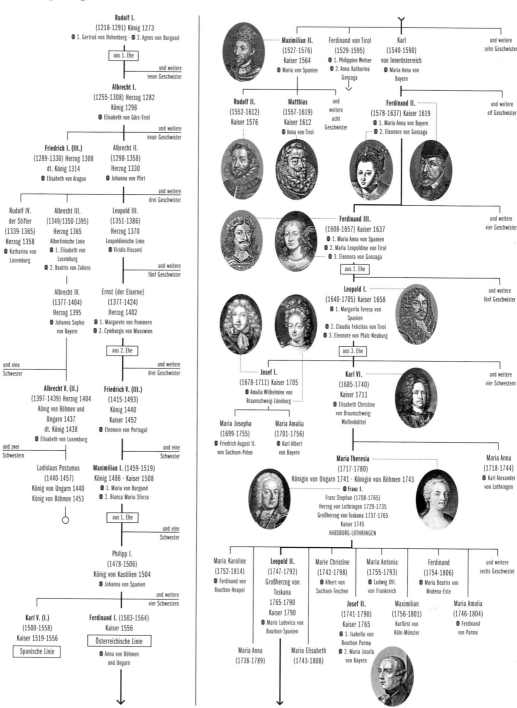

Rudolf I.
(1218-1291) König 1273
⚭ 1. Gertrud von Hohenberg · ⚭ 2. Agnes von Burgund

aus 1. Ehe

und weitere
neun Geschwister

Albrecht I.
(1255-1308) Herzog 1282
König 1298
⚭ Elisabeth von Görz-Tirol

und weitere
neun Geschwister

Friedrich I. (III.)
(1289-1330) Herzog 1308
dt. König 1314
⚭ Elisabeth von Aragon

Albrecht II.
(1298-1358)
Herzog 1330
⚭ Johanna von Pfirt

und weitere
drei Geschwister

Rudolf IV.
der Stifter
(1339-1365)
Herzog 1358
⚭ Katharina von
Luxemburg

Albrecht III.
(1349/1350-1395)
Herzog 1365
Albertinische Linie
⚭ 1. Elisabeth von
Luxemburg
⚭ 2. Beatrix von Zollern

Leopold III.
(1351-1386)
Herzog 1370
Leopoldinische Linie
⚭ Viridis Visconti

und weitere
fünf Geschwister

Albrecht IV.
(1377-1404)
Herzog 1395
⚭ Johanna Sophie
von Bayern

Ernst (der Eiserne)
(1377-1424)
Herzog 1402
⚭ 1. Margarete von Pommern
⚭ 2. Cymburgis von Masowien

aus 2. Ehe

und eine
Schwester

und weitere
drei Geschwister

Albrecht V. (II.)
(1397-1439) Herzog 1404
König von Böhmen und
Ungarn 1437
dt. König 1438
⚭ Elisabeth von Luxemburg

Friedrich V. (III.)
(1415-1493)
König 1440
Kaiser 1452
⚭ Eleonore von Portugal

und zwei
Schwestern

und eine
Schwester

Ladislaus Postumus
(1440-1457)
König von Ungarn 1440
König von Böhmen 1453

Maximilian I. (1459-1519)
König 1486 · Kaiser 1508
⚭ 1. Maria von Burgund
⚭ 2. Bianca Maria Sforza

aus 1. Ehe

und eine
Schwester

Philipp I.
(1478-1506)
König von Kastilien 1504
⚭ Johanna von Spanien

und weitere
vier Schwestern

Karl V. (I.)
(1500-1558)
Kaiser 1519-1556

Spanische Linie

Ferdinand I. (1503-1564)
Kaiser 1556

Österreichische Linie
⚭ Anna von Böhmen
und Ungarn

Maximilian II.
(1527-1576)
Kaiser 1564
⚭ Maria von Spanien

Ferdinand von Tirol
(1529-1595)
⚭ 1. Philippine Welser
⚭ 2. Anna Katharina
Gonzaga

Karl
(1540-1590)
von Innerösterreich
⚭ Maria Anna von
Bayern

und weitere
zehn Geschwister

Rudolf II.
(1552-1612)
Kaiser 1576

Matthias
(1557-1619)
Kaiser 1612
⚭ Anna von Tirol

und
weitere
acht
Geschwister

Ferdinand II.
(1578-1637) Kaiser 1619
⚭ 1. Maria Anna von Bayern
⚭ 2. Eleonore von Gonzaga

und weitere
elf Geschwister

Ferdinand III.
(1608-1657) Kaiser 1637
⚭ 1. Maria Anna von Spanien
⚭ 2. Maria Leopoldine von Tirol
⚭ 3. Eleonora von Gonzaga

und weitere
vier Geschwister

aus 1. Ehe

Leopold I.
(1640-1705) Kaiser 1658
⚭ 1. Margarita Teresa von
Spanien
⚭ 2. Claudia Felicitas von Tirol
⚭ 3. Eleonore von Pfalz-Neuburg

und weitere
fünf Geschwister

aus 3. Ehe

Josef I.
(1678-1711) Kaiser 1705
⚭ Amalia Wilhelmine von
Braunschweig-Lüneburg

Karl VI.
(1685-1740)
Kaiser 1711
⚭ Elisabeth Christine
von Braunschweig-
Wolfenbüttel

und weitere
vier Schwestern

Maria Josepha
(1699-1755)
⚭ Friedrich August II.
von Sachsen-Polen

Maria Amalia
(1701-1756)
⚭ Karl Albert
von Bayern

Maria Theresia
(1717-1780)
Königin von Ungarn 1741 · Königin von Böhmen 1743
⚭ Franz I.
Franz Stephan (1708-1765)
Herzog von Lothringen 1729-1735
Großherzog von Toskana 1737-1765
Kaiser 1745
HABSBURG-LOTHRINGEN

Maria Anna
(1718-1744)
⚭ Karl Alexander
von Lothringen

Maria Karoline
(1752-1814)
⚭ Ferdinand von
Bourbon-Neapel

Leopold II.
(1747-1792)
Großherzog von
Toskana
1765-1790
Kaiser 1790
⚭ Maria Ludovica von
Bourbon-Spanien

Marie Christine
(1742-1798)
⚭ Albert von
Sachsen-Teschen

Maria Antonia
(1755-1793)
⚭ Ludwig XVI.
von Frankreich

Josef II.
(1741-1790)
Kaiser 1765
⚭ 1. Isabella von
Bourbon Parma
⚭ 2. Maria Josefa
von Bayern

Ferdinand
(1754-1806)
⚭ Maria Beatrix von
Modena-Este

Maximilian
(1756-1801)
Kurfürst von
Köln-Münster

und weitere
sechs Geschwister

Maria Amalia
(1746-1804)
⚭ Ferdinand
von Parma

Maria Anna
(1738-1789)

Maria Elisabeth
(1743-1808)

The Habsburg Dynasty

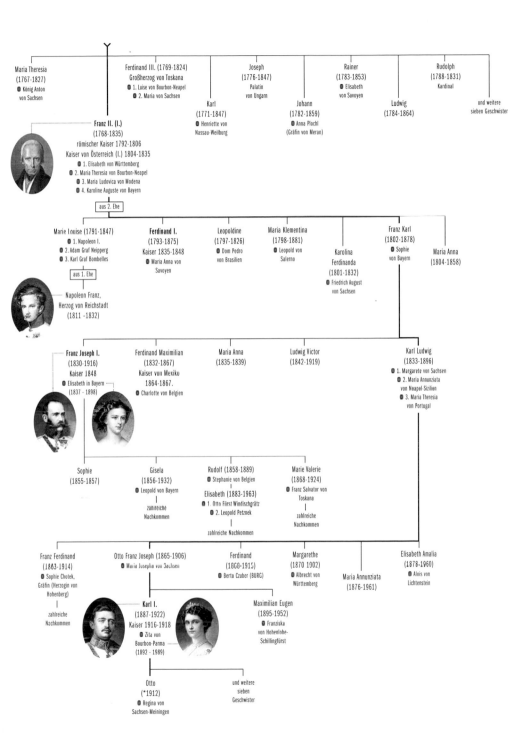

Maria Theresia
(1767-1827)
⚭ König Anton
von Sachsen

Ferdinand III. (1769-1824)
Großherzog von Toskana
⚭ 1. Luise von Bourbon-Neapel
⚭ 2. Maria von Sachsen

Karl
(1771-1847)
⚭ Henriette von
Nassau-Weilburg

Joseph
(1776-1847)
Palatin
von Ungarn

Johann
(1782-1859)
⚭ Anna Plochl
(Gräfin von Meran)

Rainer
(1783-1853)
⚭ Elisabeth
von Savoyen

Ludwig
(1784-1864)

Rudolph
(1788-1831)
Kardinal

und weitere
sieben Geschwister

Franz II. (I.)
(1768-1835)
römischer Kaiser 1792-1806
Kaiser von Österreich (I.) 1804-1835
⚭ 1. Elisabeth von Württemberg
⚭ 2. Maria Theresia von Bourbon-Neapel
⚭ 3. Maria Ludovica von Modena
⚭ 4. Karoline Auguste von Bayern

aus 2. Ehe

Marie Louise (1791-1847)
⚭ 1. Napoleon I.
⚭ 2. Adam Graf Neipperg
⚭ 3. Karl Graf Bombelles

aus 1. Ehe

Napoleon Franz,
Herzog von Reichstadt
(1811 -1832)

Ferdinand I.
(1793-1875)
Kaiser 1835-1848
⚭ Maria Anna von
Savoyen

Leopoldine
(1797-1826)
⚭ Dom Pedro
von Brasilien

Maria Klementina
(1798-1881)
⚭ Leopold von
Salerno

Karolina
Ferdinanda
(1801-1832)
⚭ Friedrich August
von Sachsen

Franz Karl
(1802-1878)
⚭ Sophie
von Bayern

Maria Anna
(1804-1858)

Franz Joseph I.
(1830-1916)
Kaiser 1848
⚭ Elisabeth in Bayern
(1837 - 1898)

Ferdinand Maximilian
(1832-1867)
Kaiser von Mexiko
1864-1867.
⚭ Charlotte von Belgien

Maria Anna
(1835-1839)

Ludwig Victor
(1842-1919)

Karl Ludwig
(1833-1896)
⚭ 1. Margarete von Sachsen
⚭ 2. Maria Annunziata
von Neapel-Sizilien
⚭ 3. Maria Theresia
von Portugal

Sophie
(1855-1857)

Gisela
(1856-1932)
⚭ Leopold von Bayern
|
zahlreiche
Nachkommen

Rudolf (1858-1889)
⚭ Stephanie von Belgien
|
Elisabeth (1883-1963)
⚭ 1. Otto Fürst Windischgrätz
⚭ 2. Leopold Petznek
|
zahlreiche Nachkommen

Marie Valerie
(1868-1924)
⚭ Franz Salvator von
Toskana
|
zahlreiche
Nachkommen

Franz Ferdinand
(1863-1914)
⚭ Sophie Chotek,
Gräfin (Herzogin von
Hohenberg)
|
zahlreiche
Nachkommen

Otto Franz Joseph (1865-1906)
⚭ Maria Josepha von Sachsen

Ferdinand
(1868-1915)
⚭ Berta Czuber (BURG)

Margarethe
(1870 1902)
⚭ Albrecht von
Württemberg

Maria Annunziata
(1876-1961)

Elisabeth Amalia
(1878-1960)
⚭ Alois von
Lichtenstein

Karl I.
(1887-1922)
Kaiser 1916-1918
⚭ Zita von
Bourbon-Parma
(1892 - 1989)

Maximilian Eugen
(1895-1952)
⚭ Franziska
von Hohenlohe-
Schillingfürst

Otto
(*1912)
⚭ Regina von
Sachsen-Meiningen

und weitere
sieben
Geschwister

From the election of Rudolf of Habsburg as Roman-German King in 1273, the House of Habsburg succeeded in establishing a powerful empire within the space of a single century. Although their efforts to secure the hereditary succession of this title for the dynasty were initially unsuccessful, a shrewd and keenly pursued policy of alliances by marriage established a solid power base, reinforcing their claims to preeminent rank, above all the title of archduke, which all members of the Habsburg dynasty bore from 1358/59 onwards.

The next Habsburg to be elected German King was Albrecht II (1437–39). In 1452 his successor to this title was crowned Holy Roman Emperor as Frederick III in Rome. From then on, the Roman-German crown remained within the House of Habsburg and later Habsburg-Lorraine until the end of the Holy Roman Empire in 1806, with a single brief interruption between 1742 and 1745, when the Wittelsbach monarch Charles VII held the title.

In 1477 Emperor Frederick III negotiated the marriage of his son Maximilian to the richest heiress of that time, Mary of Burgundy. Through this union the Habsburgs gained the territories of Burgundy and the Netherlands together with the Order of the Golden Fleece; however, it also brought an enmity with France that was to endure until well into the reign of Maria Theresa.

Maximilian I (1459–1519) continued the successful policy of matrimonial alliances. The marriage of his son, Philip the Fair, to Joan the Mad secured the Habsburgs the rich Spanish inheritance. The couple's eldest son, Emperor Charles V (1500–1558), ruled over an empire "on which the sun never set". His son, King Philip II of Spain (1527–1598), was the most powerful ruler in Europe with his overseas territories together with Burgundy, the Netherlands, Milan, Naples, Sicily and Portugal with its colonies. Charles's brother, Ferdinand (1503–1564), received the entire possessions of the Austrian patrimonial lands and the royal German crown. Through his wife, Anne, he inherited the Kingdoms of Bohemia and Hungary together with their affiliated territories. From then on, Bohemia and Hungary belonged to the Habsburg empire until the end of the Austrian monarchy in 1918.

Intended to consolidate the dynasty, the numerous matrimonial unions concluded between members of the Spanish and Austrian lines of the Habsburgs simultaneously hastened their degeneration, especially in the Spanish branch of the family.

While the Spanish Habsburgs pursued a policy with global aims, the Austrian line became encumbered with the struggle against the Turks, the travails of the Reformation and internal strife. Immortalised in a play by the famous Austrian writer Franz Grillparzer, the latter led to the splitting of the dynasty into three lines in 1564: an Austrian line, which held the imperial crown until it died out in 1619 and which moved the centre of the empire to Prague under Emperor Rudolf II, a Styrian line and a Tyrolean line. The Styrian line succeeded the other two lines which had died out, and in 1619 the imperial crown passed to Ferdinand II, who set about enforcing the Counter-Reformation in Bohemia and the Austrian lands. Following the Thirty Years' War (1618–1648) the House of Habsburg was again united in an imperial line under his grandson, Emperor Leopold I. The emperor resided at Vienna and after his great victory against the Turks in 1683 courtly life unfolded in all the splendour of the Baroque.

When the Spanish Habsburgs died out in 1700 the Austrian line was unable to retain the vast Spanish inheritance. The European powers were concerned to avoid the creation of another universal monarchy and the concentration of power that had occurred under Emperor Charles V, and so following the War of the Spanish Succession the Bourbons were installed on the Spanish throne. At the Peace of Utrecht in 1713 the Habsburgs received only the southern Netherlands, the Duchy of Milan and the kingdom of Naples and Sicily.

In order to secure this heritage, in 1713 Emperor Charles VI promulgated a decree known as the Pragmatic Sanction regulating the succession in the Habsburg dynasty: it stipulated that the undivided heritage should pass to the eldest son of the reigning emperor, and failing a son, to his eldest daughter. This also meant the separation between the emperorship and rule over the Habsburg patrimonial dominions: the Roman-German imperial crown could only pass to male heirs, while the Bohemian and Hungarian crowns could now be inherited by women. Complex negotiations with the other European powers ensued before he eventually achieved his objective with the recognition of the Pragmatic Sanction by the German imperial diet in 1732, albeit with major concessions.

Charles VI and Elisabeth Christine with their daughters Maria Theresa, Maria Anna and Maria Amalia. Watercolour miniature by Martin van Meytens, c. 1730

power in Europe. In return, the naval powers agreed to recognise and guarantee the Pragmatic Sanction.

Emperor Charles VI was a thoroughly Baroque ruler, and during his reign (1711–1740) the Baroque age in Austria came to full flower. Besides the crown of the Holy Roman Empire he bore the royal crowns of Bohemia, Hungary, Croatia and Naples. His reign was marked by the wars against the Turks, which under the capable generalship of Prince Eugene of Savoy

Although the emperorship was the highest dignity and a sonorous title, the real power was concentrated in the rule of the sovereign who attempted to weld this conglomerate of heterogeneous and inherited territories into a centrally ruled state.

At the Viennese court, hope of a male heir had not been abandoned, and in April 1716, a son was born to Charles VI and his wife, Elisabeth Christine of Brunswick-Wolfenbüttel. Baptised with the name of Leopold, the infant died in November of the same year, however. Maria Theresa was born in 1717, followed by two further daughters, Maria Anna and Maria Amalie, the latter dying at the age of six. Charles VI now secretly pledged to give the hand of his first-born daughter only to a prince of inferior power in order not to disturb the balance of

Emperor Charles VI. Oil painting by Johann Gottfried Auerbach, c. 1735

resulted in the acquisition of the Banat, part of northern Serbia with Belgrade and Bosnia, and also Walachia Minor and thus led to the greatest south-eastern expansion of the Austrian monarchy in the Balkans.

As a result of the War of the Polish Succession the emperor was forced to cede Naples and Sicily in 1735, and his future son-in-law, Franz Stephan of Lorraine, had to relinquish his patrimonial lands of Lorraine and Barrois, which were occupied by France. This was the situation in the empire and the Habsburg dominions when Charles VI died suddenly on 20 October 1740, leaving his young and largely unprepared daughter as his successor. His reign had centred on the question of the succession in the empire and the Austrian patrimonial lands. Just how fragile the guarantees of the Pragmatic Sanction by the European powers were would be demonstrated by Maria Theresa's accession to power.

Empress Elisabeth Christine. Oil painting. Anonymous, c. 1735

Childhood to marriage

Maria Theresa was born in the Vienna Hofburg on 13 May 1717. Her parents, Emperor Charles VI and Empress Elisabeth Christine, seem to have enjoyed a harmonious marriage but their happiness was overshadowed by the lack of a male heir. Elisabeth Christine had to endure numerous 'miracle cures' held to be conducive to conception. Right up to the end of his life the emperor still held out hope of an heir to the throne and his two daughters were kept very much in the background. Thus Maria Theresa enjoyed a carefree childhood away from the formalities of court life, growing into beautiful young girl whose graceful demeanour charmed all around her. She was blonde, healthy and cheerful, with a frank and generous disposition. With all the vivacity of youth the archduchess participated enthusiastically in celebrations and masked balls, dancing tirelessly into the small hours.

Archduchess Maria Theresa at the age of three. Oil painting. Anonymous, c. 1720

Maria Theresa received an education that was appropriate to her rank but did not include anything out of the ordinary to prepare her for her future role as heiress of the Austrian crown lands. Educated by Jesuits, she learned Latin, Spanish, Italian and French; she spoke German only as Viennese dialect. Like any other child of her rank, the young princess learned to make music and to dance, demonstrating a particular talent for singing. Her Jesuit priest tutors naturally also taught her religious knowledge: Catholicism was an integral part of the Habsburg identity and in its doctrine of the divine right of kings legitimised their claim to power. At the age of eleven Maria Theresa's upbringing was entrusted to the widowed Countess Charlotte Fuchs. She encouraged her charge's early affection for Franz Stephan of Lorraine, who arrived at the Viennese court aged fifteen in June 1723. The houses of Lorraine and Habsburg were related, and the young duke had been sent to his uncle's court to acquire a cosmopolitan education. Soon after being presented to the emperor in Prague he accompanied him on court hunting excursions. He shared Charles VI's passion for the chase and not least for this reason immediately secured the emperor's affection. Within a short time the emperor had unofficially promised his father, Duke Leopold I of Lorraine, who was also his cousin, that his son could marry Maria Theresa, at that time just six years old.

Archduchess Maria Theresa at the age of 12. Oil painting by Andreas Möller, c. 1729

Countess Maria Karolina Fuchs, Maria Theresa's governess. Oil painting. Anonymous, c. 1745

Franz Stephan of Lorraine at the age of 15 in hunting dress. Oil painting. Anonymous, c. 1723

While Franz Stephan was at first merely a playmate for the little Maria Theresa, as the princess entered her teenage years she began to develop a deep affection for the duke, and when he left the court in 1729 in order to assume the regency in Lorraine, the twelve-year-old archduchess was inconsolable.

Despite the promise he had made, Charles VI initially regarded the developing relationship with misgivings: Franz Stephan was not an imperial prince and his inheritance, the Duchy of Lorraine and Barrois, was the object of political claims by other European princely houses, and was in fact eventually to be lost to France in the War of the Polish Succession in 1736. In recompense, Franz Stephan was promised the Grand Duchy of Tuscany after the death of the last regent without issue, Gian Gastone de Medici.

Following a period of extensive travel across Europe, Franz Stephan, now virtually landless, returned to Vienna in 1732. Maria Theresa's childish crush grew into a tempestuous love, and with Charles VI's permission, the official betrothal took place on 21 January 1736. After this the duke withdrew to Pressburg (modern-day Bratislava), where he was to remain until the wedding on 12 February. Letters that passed between the bridal couple during this time have been preserved and attest to the tender and ardent affection they cherished for one another. Franz Stephan was to remain the love of Maria Theresa's life.

Although it was more than likely that Maria Theresa would inherit the Habsburg lands, Charles VI did not make his daughter, now married, familiar with affairs of state in any way – he had evidently still not given up hope of a male heir. It was probably under the influence of Franz Stephan, who was critical of the circumspect way the emperor ruled, that the young archduchess had her first insights into the world of politics. Her growing awareness of the likelihood that she would have to assume the reins of state at some point in the future helped Maria Theresa to form her own, equally critical opinions during this time, as the English ambassador Sir Thomas Robinson reported in 1733: "She is a princess of the highest spirit; her father's losses are her own; she admires his virtues but condemns his mismanagement; and is of a temper so formed for rule and ambition as to look upon him as little more than her administrator."

MARIE THERESE
Imperatrice des Romains,
Reine de Hongrie & de Bohême
Archiduchesse d'Autriche &c &c &c.

Maria Theresa in a medallion with double eagle and insignia. Copperplate engraving by Johann Elias Ridinger, c. 1740

When Charles VI died suddenly following a hunting excursion at Halbthurn in 1740, his 23-year-old daughter came into an inheritance fraught with difficulties; surrounded by her father's mostly elderly advisors, she realised that all his efforts to have the Pragmatic Sanction recognised had been in vain and she was faced with a battle for the Austrian succession. Thus the first task of the young monarch was to defend and secure her heritage.

Maria Theresa's policies

Emperor Charles VI left his daughter an empire that extended over a vast territory but which had undergone a considerable decline in economic, military and administrative terms.

The prince-electors of Bavaria and Saxony, who were married to the daughters of Joseph I, Maria Theresa's uncle, laid immediate claim to the Austrian succession following the death of Charles VI, declaring their previous relinquishment of the succession to be void. To the north a further threat loomed in the person of the young King Frederick II of Prussia, who had just come to power. In contrast to Maria Theresa, he had inherited full coffers and a powerful, well-organised army. Frederick exploited Maria Theresa's weak position, demanding the prosperous duchy of Silesia on the basis of prior claims. Only if Silesia was ceded to him would he recognise the Pragmatic Sanction.

In October 1740 Prussian troops marched into Silesia, to be welcomed by the predominantly Protestant population. The Prussians' rapid advance encouraged the other powers to strike. Bavaria, supported by French troops, Saxony and Spain attacked – the War of the Austrian Succession had begun, a conflict that was to last until 1748.

Queen of Hungary and Bohemia

In this critical situation the young and beautiful Maria Theresa won the sympathies of the Hungarian nobility and support from the Hungarian imperial diet in Pressburg which placed a contingent of troops at her disposal. In return she promised to respect the Hungarian constitution. With Hungarian support Austrian forces expelled the Bavarians from Upper Austria and in June 1741 Maria Theresa was crowned Queen of Hungary at Pressburg.

Maria Theresa as Queen of Hungary on the coronation mound at Pressburg.
Copperplate engraving by Johann Elias Ridinger, 1741

In the meantime, Bavarian troops supported by French forces reoccupied Upper Austria and parts of Lower Austria, later marching against Prague, where the Bavarian prince-elector Karl Albert had himself crowned King of Bohemia. Shortly afterwards, at the beginning of 1742, he was also elected Roman-German emperor in Frankfurt as Charles VII – the first time for 304 years that this title had not been vested in a member of the house of Habsburg.

Soon afterwards the Prussian army launched new offensives, and when the Austrian army was defeated, Maria Theresa was compelled to give up most of Silesia at the Peace of Breslau in 1742. However, this meant that she could now concentrate her military potential on the other theatres of war.

With Hungarian support the Bavarian and French troops were finally driven from the Austrian patrimonial lands.

The Ladies' Carousel

Maria Theresa celebrated the retaking of Prague from the Bavarians with a Ladies' Carousel in the winter riding school of the Vienna Hofburg on 2 January 1743, an event that was recorded in an oil painting by the court artist Martin van Meytens and his studio. The participants – ladies from the highest aristocratic circles – were dressed as "Amazons". In the arena of the riding school figures with clay heads were set up which had to be knocked off with a

The Ladies' Carousel in the Winter Riding School in January 1743. Oil painting by Martin van Meytens and studio

lance by the riders and with a sword by those driving the carriages. Mounted on a grey, Maria Theresa led the first quadrille of riders which was followed by three further quadrilles, the second also mounted and the other two composed of small shell-shaped carriages called phaetons. The spectators were impressed by this magnificent display, the opulent costumes worn by the ladies and the rich harnesses of their steeds. From the stands the courtiers and invited guests could admire the skill of the ladies which were in no way inferior to those of a practised cavalier, as noted in the report of the event carried by the *Wiener Diarium*, and successful participants were rewarded with valuable prizes. After the event Maria Theresa repaired to the Hofburg, where the celebration concluded with a magnificent ball.

In the following spring Maria Theresa celebrated her triumphal entry into Prague and was crowned Queen of Bohemia in St Vitus' Cathedral on 13 May, her 26th birthday. She had triumphed over her enemies, defended the Habsburg dominions and had strengthened her hold on her inheritance. Her return to Vienna was also a triumph; the young monarch had conquered the hearts of her people.

Imperial dignity for Habsburg-Lorraine

In the meantime Emperor Charles VII had died suddenly in 1745, and after his son had relinquished all his hereditary claims in Austria and to the imperial crown, nothing more stood in the way of Maria Theresa's husband, Franz Stephan of Lorraine, Grand Duke of Tuscany, becoming emperor. He was elected by the majority of the prince-electors and crowned Roman-German emperor as Francis I in Frankfurt on 4 October 1745. Thus the imperial crown was once again in the hands of the House of Habsburg-Lorraine.

Although she was present at the ceremony in Frankfurt, Maria Theresa was not crowned empress.

Immediately after the coronation the struggle for Silesia and Bohemia was renewed, ending in heavy defeats for Austria. In the course of the subsequent peace negotiations Maria Theresa was forced to cede Silesia to Frederick II in return for the latter's recognition of Franz Stephan as Roman-German emperor. Although this put an end to the war of succession within the empire, military conflict continued as a war of the European coalitions based on the rivalry between France and Britain in Europe and the colonies.

Banquet held on the occasion of the coronation of Franz Stephan of Lorraine as Roman-German emperor at Frankfurt in 1745.
Copperplate engraving by I. G. Funck, I. N. Lentzner and W. C. Mayr, 1746

The Peace of Aachen in 1748 brought the War of the Austrian Succession to a final conclusion for Maria Theresa, with international recognition of the Pragmatic Sanction and thus the hereditary succession of the House of Habsburg-Lorraine. The terms of the peace treaty compelled her to cede the duchies of Parma, Piacenza and Guastalla to the Spanish Bourbons, while the southern Netherlands were returned to Austrian rule. Despite considerable losses of territory, Maria Theresa had held her own, showing herself to be a ruler of courage and perspicacity.

The reform of the empire

In the years that followed up to the outbreak of the Seven Years' War in 1756 Maria Theresa devoted herself to domestic policies, beginning with a reorganisation of the monarchy with the aim of reforming the army, the financial system and the administration.

Her most important ally in this task was the Silesian count Friedrich Wilhelm von Haugwitz, who implemented a modified administrative and fiscal system based on French and Prussian models against the opposition of the powerful provincial estates in the western part of the Habsburg monarchy. The merging of the group of Bohemian and Austrian provinces into a centralised and absolutist state and the removal of the provincial estates from the political and fiscal administration characterised the monarchy until its dissolution in 1918.

The reform of the financial and fiscal system began in 1749 with the introduction of a new financial and administrative authority. Church and nobility were no longer exempt from taxes, land tax was calculated on the basis of the size of the property and paper money introduced.

Entrusted with the implementation of the administrative reform, Haugwitz created the *Directorium in publicis et cameralibus* as the supreme political and fiscal authority. Subordinate to this were the *Gubernien* (governorships), while the lowest level of administrative authority were the *Kreisämter* or district offices. The latter were responsible for collecting taxes and were better able to control the local estates. The reforms naturally encountered considerable resistance from the nobility, which saw them as an unacceptable curtailment of its freedoms, but the measures were implemented despite their opposition.

Maria Theresa in a fur-trimmed gown. Pastel on vellum by Jean Étienne Liotard, 1743

Maria Theresa had a great ability to surround herself with distinguished enlightened advisors and ministers under whose influence and supervision major social and educational reforms were introduced. These included penal law, with the abolition of torture, measures to promote crafts, small trades, manufacture and trade, and the abolition of rural serfdom. Further achievements dating from shortly after 1750 included the reform of the entire educational system from elementary schools to universities, management of property held by the church and the monasteries, poor relief, the organisation of dioceses and parishes, the numbers of priests and a reduction in the number of religious holidays.

The reform of the administration went hand in hand with reform of the army, which was carried out by Count Leopold Joseph von Daun. The utilisation and organisation of the state's military power was the most important leitmotiv in Maria Theresa's domestic policy. She never came to terms with the loss of Silesia, which had been the most productive and prosperous of the Austrian provinces. The retaking of this region and the exclusion of Prussia from the circle of the Great Powers was her supreme goal, and in this respect the reforms implemented by Haugwitz were primarily intended to increase the military striking power of the Habsburg empire.

The empress herself frequently attended military exercises. Count Daun, later commander in chief during the Seven Years' War, issued service regulations for the army. Lighter, manoeuvrable and rapid-firing cannon were developed, and in 1752 the empress founded a military academy at Wiener Neustadt, an institution that still exists today.

Foreign policy conducted with diplomatic skill

While the reform of the state and the army dominated domestic politics, foreign policy underwent a general reorientation under the auspices of Count (from 1764 Prince) Wenzel Anton von Kaunitz which was to determine Austrian foreign policy for the entire second half of the 18th century. For more than 40 years he controlled foreign affairs and to an increasing extent domestic policies as well. He was appointed court and state chancellor in 1753, and at the Privy Conference, the supreme advisory council of the monarch, he was a proponent of reconciliation between Austria and France right from the beginning, thus initiating a complete reversal of the foreign policy pursued by the Habsburgs for the previous two and a half centuries that would ultimately be reflected in the marriage alliances chosen by Maria Theresa for her children.

The hereditary enmity with France, which had always striven to resist being hemmed in by the Habsburg powers of Spain, the Holy Roman Empire and Burgundy and had often allied itself with the enemies of the Habsburgs such as the Turks, had diminished since the end of the War of the Spanish Succession. Against the will of Emperor Franz Stephan, who wanted to maintain the alliance with Britain, but in complete concord with the empress, Kaunitz engineered what came to be known as the *"renversement des alliances"*, first in his role as envoy in Paris and from 1753 as state chancellor. Following protracted negotiations the treaty between Austria and France was signed at Versailles on 1 May 1756.

Sweden and Saxony were also persuaded to join the alliance against Frederick II. Austria had entered into a defensive alliance with Russia several years previously, Tsarina Elizabeth I being a vehement opponent of the Prussian ruler.

The Seven Years' War

In this situation Frederick II seized the initiative and invaded Saxony. The Seven Years' War that ensued as a result of this attack by Prussia brought Maria Theresa both victories and defeats. After Prussian forces had besieged Prague, an Austrian army under the command of Field Marshal Count Leopold Daun defeated the Prussians at Kolin on 18 June 1757. Maria Theresa later referred to this event as the "birth of the monarchy". To mark this victory against her greatest adversary she established the Order of Maria Theresa, Austria's highest military order, investing Field Marshal Daun with its Grand Cross. The first investiture of the order, of Daun and Charles of Lorraine, was recorded in a painting by Martin van Meytens which today still hangs in the palace at Schönbrunn.

The first awarding of the Order of Maria Theresa by Franz I Stephan to Count Daun in 1758.
Oil painting by Martin van Meytens and studio

Following the death of Tsarina Elizabeth, who was succeeded by Tsar Peter II and his wife, Catherine II, Russia changed its policy towards Prussia. Like Britain and France, the Russian tsar wanted peace with Frederick II, and through the mediation of Saxony the peace treaty of Hubertusberg was signed between Austria and Prussia on 15 February 1763. For the third and final time Austria relinquished its claim to Silesia and in return received the consent of Frederick II to the election as Holy Roman Emperor of Maria Theresa's son, Crown Prince Joseph, who was crowned Roman-German king in the following year. The Seven Years' War had confirmed the emergence of Prussia as a major European power and established a new balance of power between Britain, France, Austria, Prussia and Russia.

To mark the coronation of the crown prince at Frankfurt in October 1764 and the securing of the imperial title for the House of Habsburg-Lorraine, Maria Theresa established a second order. Known as the Order of St Stephen, it was the first order of civil merit created in the monarchy. Named after the patron saint of Hungary and originally intended for the Kingdom of Hungary, it became the most distinguished order of merit in the monarchy for outstanding, non-military services rendered to the state. The first investiture of the order held in the Vienna Hofburg on 6 May 1764 was recorded by Martin van Meytens and shows Maria Theresa as Queen of Hungary awarding the order to several candidates, including her personal physician, Gerard van Swieten.

Banquet held on the occasion of the coronation of Franz Stephan of Lorraine as Roman-German emperor at Frankfurt in 1764. Oil painting by Martin van Meytens and studio

The first investiture ceremony of the Order of St Stephen on 6 May 1764 in the Ritterstube of the Vienna Hofburg. Oil painting by Martin van Meytens and studio

The policies of the widow and her co-ruler

With the sudden death of Franz Stephan in 1765 during the wedding celebrations for Archduke Leopold, the future Grand Duke of Tuscany, at Innsbruck, Joseph II became the co-ruler with Maria Theresa in the Austrian hereditary lands and succeeded to the title of emperor. The following fifteen years were marked by tensions between mother and son which resulted from the differences in both their characters and their ideas about foreign and domestic policies.

After peace had been concluded with Prussia, Maria Theresa's political actions were determined by her resolve to maintain peace for her peoples. When Poland was divided up between Russia, Prussia and Austria, she had to bow to the plans and decisions of her son, who had made approaches to Frederick II against her will. In order to maintain the peace she even

Joseph II. Oil painting by the circle of Martin van Meytens, c. 1765

went so far in the question of the Bavarian succession in 1777 as to write to her arch-enemy Frederick to solicit a peaceful solution. However, Maria Theresa would not live to see the conclusion of the peace treaty: the great monarch died on 29 November 1780 after a reign of forty years.

Despite their numerous political and military clashes the Prussian king had the greatest respect for his adversary. In 1781, a year after her death, he wrote: "She did honour to her throne and her sex; I waged war with her, but I was never her enemy".

Theresa's Last Day; *Maria Theresa on her deathbed, surrounded by her children Maria Elisabeth, Joseph II, Maximilian, Albert of Saxony, Maria Anna and Marie Christine. Copperplate engraving by Johann Hieronymus Löschenkohl, 1780*

Frederick the Great, King of Prussia. Detail from a copperplate engraving by I. E. Nilson after Aug. Vind., 1763

divine right of kings, she saw her dominion and power as divinely sanctioned and thus felt responsible to God and her people. Sustained by this responsibility, she insisted on her subjects adopting the Catholic religion to the exclusion of all other faiths. In contrast to her predecessors, however, she made a distinction between her faith and the established church, of which she was critical.

All her life, she remained opposed to the ideas of the Enlightenment to which her son, Emperor Joseph II, subscribed, and yet she introduced many reforms that today we recognise as exemplifying enlightened absolutism.

As was traditional in the Habsburg dynasty, Maria Theresa's beliefs were deeply rooted in the Catholic faith, which constituted the fundament of her political and personal actions. In keeping with the notion of the

The imperial family

Emperor and empress – an unusual couple with a clear division of roles

The indisputable centre of Maria Theresa's private life was her consort, Franz Stephan, who had been elected Roman-German emperor through the political adroitness of his wife. As he showed no particular ambition in political terms his young wife and monarch gradually took over the political business of the empire while her husband devoted his energies to the economic challenges of the monarchy. Although Franz Stephan remained in Maria Theresa's shadow as far as politics were concerned, he earned a reputation throughout Europe as a financial and economic expert, restoring the budget of the empire and at the same time considerably increasing the personal fortune of the Habsburgs. He spent his leisure time hunting and playing cards, either alone or with the empress and/or in the society of the court.

Maria Theresa as Queen of Hungary. Oil painting by Martin van Meytens, c. 1750/55

Franz I Stephan of Lorraine in uniform wearing the Order of Maria Theresa. Pastel by Jean Étienne Liotard, c. 1748

Maria Theresa, at the age of around 30. Oil painting after J. E. Liotard, attributed to Marie Christine, c. 1748/50

Maria Theresa idolised her husband but was extremely possessive, a situation which inevitably led to jealousy, given her husband's predilections.

Despite her many political tasks Maria Theresa did not neglect her private life and made her family a central part of her life. Apart from Franz Stephan's weakness for the female sex and the resulting jealousy on the part of the empress, the imperial couple's marriage was harmonious and blessed with many children.

Increasing almost annually, their brood of children gave life at court a youthful cheerfulness, *joie de vivre* and presumably a certain degree of naturalness. Around 1760 the Viennese court was regarded as one of the most attractive in Europe. Prince Albert of Saxony, later to become one of Maria Theresa's sons-in-law, wrote on first visiting the imperial family: "There is no more charming sight than the long line of the family as they follow behind their illustrious parents at public church ceremonies".

Within a space of twenty years, between the ages of 19 and 38, Maria Theresa bore sixteen children, of whom four sons and six daughters survived into adulthood. Two children died shortly after birth, the eldest daughter in infancy, while two daughters and a son died of smallpox and an acute fever respectively.

Maria Theresa loved her children dearly, but had the responsible and difficult task of providing for them in a style appropriate to their station in life and also of negotiating advantageous matches for them in order to secure the empire. Maria Theresa thus pursued a deliberate marriage policy to which all her children were all bound to submit – with the exception of her favourite daughter, Marie Christine.

Franz I Stephan and Maria Theresa surrounded by their family. Copperplate engraving by J. M. Probst, c. 1760

Numerous letters written by her children in later years, when they were living at various princely courts around Europe, reveal that this maternal care for the wellbeing of her children was not always appreciated, and that her love for her children was often not reciprocated. Right into adulthood and even when living far from the court at Vienna, most of her children feared their domineering and resolute mother. However, this did not preclude them from also having the greatest respect for her.

Right from the start of her reign in 1740 Maria Theresa endeavoured to draw up a personal plan for her daily routine, so that she could devote equal amounts of time to the affairs of government and to the family. Both parents felt responsible for maintaining family life, the central focus of which was the upbringing and education of their numerous progeny.

Maria Theresa as monarch in a lace-trimmed gown. Oil painting by Martin van Meytens, c. 1750/55

Maria Anna, Marie Christine and Maria Elisabeth on an ermine fur. Oil painting by Martin van Meytens, c. 1744

Maria Theresa had very definite ideas of what constituted an appropriate upbringing and these notions informed the instructions given to the children's *aios* and *aias*, as their principal tutors and governesses were called. The smallest children, born soon after one another, were all put in the *Kindskammer* or imperial nursery, where they were looked after by a lady-in-waiting and her attendants. From the age of five each child was given its own suite of rooms, and in the case of the young archdukes, female staff were replaced by male attendants. In addition to the child's *aio*, several tutors and a personal father confessor assumed responsibility for the child's education. They received their own household at the age of fifteen if they had not already married and left the Viennese court by then. Maria Theresa and Franz Stephan encouraged good relationships among their children, and later on, when the children had married and were living at courts all over Europe, their mother ensured that they continued to visit and support one another.

Franz I Stephan and Maria Theresa surrounded by their family. Oil painting by Martin van Meytens, c. 1754/55

Neither Maria Theresa nor Franz Stephan liked strict court etiquette, preferring a more relaxed atmosphere both within the family circle and on official occasions and visits. Thus they achieved a combination of imperial pomp and private family life that was unusual for that time.

Upbringing and education

Both the emperor and empress were concerned to give their children an appropriate upbringing and education. Their tutors were carefully chosen and were given elaborate instructions; even the timetables were drawn up in collaboration with the imperial couple. The progress made by the children was carefully monitored and discussed at regular meetings with the tutors and the child's *aio* or *aia*. The individuals responsible for the children's upbringing and education were instructed to show understanding for the child's individual character and to promote his or her special talents. Taking the latter into account, lessons were to be taught in such a way that made the subject interesting for the child.

The choice of individuals for the upbringing and education of their children lay in the hands of the parents, and they often had difficulties in finding and above all keeping suitable personnel that met their requirements. Thus for example the *aia* of their daughter Maria Amalia was relieved of her post; Maria Theresa felt that she was too strict for the personal development of her shy and rather introverted daughter, even though she propagated obedience as one of the foremost virtues.

The children's education was based on the *Fürstenspiegel*, a popular work written for children of the nobility which contained practical advice and clearly defined aims for their upbringing and education. It placed the greatest emphasis on the formation of character, which Maria Theresa also held to be of utmost importance, given that her sons were being educated to be good rulers.

In addition to general knowledge, their education also included instruction in special subjects according to the path that had been chosen for each child. For example, as the future bride of the French king, Maria Antonia was given careful instruction in dancing and etiquette, as these were of foremost importance at the Versailles court.

The boys' education was supplemented by military training by which Maria Theresa set great store. However, she was disappointed that the young archdukes' interest in military matters was very limited, even though they had all been appointed regimental commanders at the age of five or six.

The three eldest sons of the imperial couple: Joseph (centre), Karl Joseph (right) and Peter Leopold (left) as regimental commanders-in-chief. Oil painting by Martin van Meytens, c. 1755

Maria Theresa in Turkish costume with a mask. Oil painting by Martin van Meytens, c. 1745

Girl with a flute. Watercolour, signed Maria Anna, *c. 1755*

The children's formal education was divided into two phases. The first phase covered basic skills with reading and writing, Latin, foreign languages, history, geography, land surveying, military architecture, mathematics, music, dancing and gymnastics. Religious knowledge was taught two years before their general education began. The second phase, from the ages of fourteen to seventeen, was devoted to higher studies and included metaphysics, logic, rhetoric, mathematics, law, history and languages.

In addition to these subjects the parents also paid great attention to their children's artistic and musical education, no doubt on account of their own predilections. Maria Theresa herself had been an enthusiastic dancer in her youth and had displayed a special talent for singing. All the children were taught to make music and to dance; the girls were given singing lessons and the boys learnt to play instruments. In 1747 a special theatre was constructed at Schönbrunn and ceremonially opened on the emperor's name-day with a performance given by the children. Numerous balls, masked dances and other celebrations at which the imperial children and courtiers took to the stage and the populace formed the audience were often recorded in paintings and engravings. Christenings, investitures, weddings, children's masked parties – the calendar of the imperial family and the Viennese court was full of such events which were used by the imperial couple with their swarm of children to enhance the pomp and standing of the court.

Drawing and painting were also on the children's timetable, with the daughters displaying a particular talent in this field. Together with their equally talented father, they produced numerous artistic works, some of which were used to decorate the imperial apartments at Schönbrunn. All in all, the subject-matter taught was wide-ranging and difficult to assimilate, and the children were busy with their daily programme of tuition from morning to evening. Not until the evening did the family meet to spend time playing games and dancing together.

Young lady with hat. Watercolour, signed Elisabeth, *c. 1755*

Actors performing in the city. Watercolour, signed Franz Stephan, *c. 1755*

The Porcelain Room at Schönbrunn Palace, decorated with numerous pen-and-ink drawings executed by members of the imperial family

It was only natural that quarrels and petty jealousies constantly arose between the children, especially as Maria Theresa did not treat them equally, favouring some of them over the others. Franz Stephan on the other hand was the one who treated all his children with equal kindness and warmth, always endeavouring to maintain a harmonious atmosphere within the family. He also encouraged the children who were treated unfairly by their mother (Maria Anna, Maria Amalia and Ferdinand), protecting them from persecution by their siblings.

The death of Franz Stephan

In August 1765 the Viennese court travelled to Innsbruck for the wedding of the imperial couple's second-eldest son, Peter Leopold, to the Spanish infanta Maria Ludovica of Bourbon, the daughter of Charles III of Spain. The ceremony took place on 5 August and was accompanied by numerous celebrations extending over several days. Following a visit to the theatre on the evening of 18 August Franz Stephan returned to his apartments in the Innsbruck Hofburg. After bidding his son Joseph good night he suddenly stopped and leaned his head against the wall. Joseph hurried back to support him. The emperor sank to the ground and even the physicians who had been immediately summoned could do nothing to help him. Franz Stephan had suffered a stroke which killed him at the age of 57. The sudden death of her husband was a bitter blow for Maria Theresa; for days she shut herself up in her apartments, speaking to nobody. She had the room where Franz Stephan had died transformed into a chapel in which a mass in his memory is still celebrated today on the anniversary of his death. Maria Theresa subsequently distributed her jewellery among her children, gave all her colourful gowns to her ladies-in-waiting and wore mourning for the rest of her life. After the empress's death a piece of paper was found in her prayer book on which she had made a precise note of the duration of her happy marriage, even taking leap years into account: "29 years, 6 months, 6 days, equals 29 years, 335 months, 1540 weeks, 10,781 days, 258,744 hours."

Franz Stephan had always been the centre of Maria Theresa's life. In him she found solace and support for her cares, and with him she shared the joys of her existence. His death left a void which could not be filled. She wrote to her friend, Countess Edling in Gorizia: "I have lost the kindest of men … he was the whole solace of my hard existence".

Maria Theresa in widowhood. Oil painting by Anton von Maron, c. 1768/70

The death of the emperor also had consequences for life at court: from then on ladies had to dress in black, and the wearing of cosmetics was prohibited. Maria Theresa moved out of the apartments she had shared with her husband in the Leopoldine Wing of the Hofburg and took up residence in a new apartment on the second floor. At Schönbrunn Palace the *Retirade* of the late emperor was remodelled as a memorial room with precious Chinese lacquer panels. Known today as the Vieux-Laque Room, it is still one of the most important interiors from the time of Maria Theresa.

The Vieux-Laque Room at Schönbrunn Palace

The children of the imperial couple

Maria Elisabeth (1737–1740)

Maria Anna, also called Marianne (1738–1789), was born with a slight deformity and was a sickly child. The preferential treatment given to her other siblings induced her to try to make herself the centre of attention. She made herself unpopular with those around her, treating them with a mixture of arrogance and envy. She felt closest to her father, with whom she shared an interest in the natural sciences, particularly in mineralogy and numismatics. Like her father, she was a talented draughtswoman and also exhibited a gift for acting. Her artistic ambitions – drawing, watercolour painting and copperplate engraving – were recognised when she enrolled in the newly-established Copperplate Engraving Academy in Vienna in 1767 and two years later in the Grand-Ducal Academy of Arts at Florence. Together with her teacher, Ignaz von Born, an important scholar who introduced her to Masonic circles, she assembled a mineralogical collection which is today held at the Natural History Museum in Vienna. She also compiled a magnificent volume on the medals of the age of Maria Theresa which is today preserved in the Coin Cabinet of the Kunsthistorisches Museum. Unmarried and from 1766 the nominal abbess of a noblewomen's order in Prague, she lived at the court in Vienna until her mother's death. In 1781 she was removed from the court by her brother, Joseph II, and subsequently lived at Klagenfurt near the Convent of the Order of St Elizabeth, where she surrounded herself with individuals who shared her interest in the natural sciences and art.

Maria Anna. Oil painting by the Master of the Archduchess Portraits, c. 1762/65

Portrait of an Arab. Watercolour, signed Maria Anna, c. 1755

Marie Karoline (1740–1741)

Joseph (1741–1790) was born amid the turmoil of the War of Succession, after three daughters, two of whom had already died. Maria Theresa and Franz Stephan were naturally overjoyed at the birth of a male heir. Separated from his sisters and surrounded only by ladies-

Crown Prince Joseph in the uniform of a Hungarian magnate, aged two. Oil painting by Martin van Meytens, c. 1743

in-waiting, Joseph was thoroughly spoilt during his early childhood. In 1748 The Hungarian field marshal Count Karl von Batthyány was appointed *aio* to the crown prince in order to correct the mistakes that had been made in his upbringing, for which Maria Theresa was partly responsible. Joseph was taught a wide range of subjects and examined four times a year, but his mother remained dissatisfied with his progress. She instructed the head of the state chancellery, Johann Christoph von Bartenstein, to elaborate guidelines for Joseph's studies in order to give him the best possible preparation for his future role as ruler. Bartenstein showed an adroit hand in the choice of his tutors: the Thuringian scholar Christian August Beck, professor of state and feudal law at the Theresianum in Vienna, introduced the crown prince to Enlightenment teachings which had an enduring influence on his views. Beck advocated religious tolerance and the abolition of torture and serfdom. In keeping with family

tradition, the crown prince had to learn a trade; significantly, Joseph decided on the craft of book-printing.

As crown prince, Joseph had a privileged position among his siblings within the family. He was felt to be spoilt and arrogant, and it was his siblings who were closest to him in age in particular who bore the brunt of his exaggerated self-confidence and sarcasm. He showed a more caring side of his character towards his younger siblings; he was admired by Maria Antonia, and was a role model for his youngest brother, Maximilian Franz.

Joseph as a young boy. Oil painting attributed to Martin van Meytens, c. 1765

In the middle of the Seven Years' War against the Prussian king Frederick II, which had been triggered by an alliance between the Habsburgs and their erstwhile arch-enemy France in 1756, the politically-motivated marriage of the crown prince to Isabella of Bourbon-Parma took place. Although Parma was a politically insignificant principality, Isabella's mother was the favourite daughter of the French king Louis XV, and Isabella herself, famed for her beauty and intelligence, a brilliant match. The elaborate marriage celebrations took place over several days in October 1760 and were recorded by the court artist Martin van Meytens and his studio in a series of large-scale paintings

Isabella of Parma, wife of Crown Prince Joseph. Copperplate engraving by J. E. Nilson, c. 1760

Wedding Cycle in the Hall of Ceremonies at Schönbrunn Palace: The Entry of the Bride. Oil painting by Martin van Meytens and studio, 1760/65

The Wedding Ceremony in the Church of the Augustine Friars. Oil painting by Martin van Meytens and studio, 1760/65

Court Banquet in the Great Anticamera of the Vienna Hofburg. Oil painting by Martin van Meytens and studio, 1760/65

Souper in the Redoute Halls. Oil painting by Martin van Meytens and studio, 1760/65

Serenade in the Redoute Hall. Oil painting by Martin van Meytens and studio, 1760/65

Isabella of Parma, wife of Crown Prince Joseph. Oil painting attributed to Marie Christine, c. 1760

Josefa of Bavaria, second wife of Crown Prince Joseph. Oil painting. Anonymous, c. 1765

that were incorporated into the décor of the Hall of Ceremonies at Schönbrunn in 1776/78.

Joseph worshipped his wife, but she did not return his love, developing instead a great affection for Marie Christine, the crown prince's sister. Under constant pressure to produce a male heir, Isabella was unhappy and discontented at the Viennese court. After bearing a daughter who was baptised Maria Theresia (1762–1770) she suffered three miscarriages. Only a few days after being delivered of a second daughter, who died shortly after her birth, Isabella fell victim to one of the smallpox epidemics that recurred regularly in Vienna and died, aged just twenty-two.

Joseph never got over this heavy blow and from this time on dedicated himself exclusively to a single task: the well-being of the state. Nonetheless, Maria Theresa planned a second, politically-motivated marriage for her first-born son, her choice falling on Josefa of Bavaria. Despite vehement opposition from Joseph, the marriage took place in January 1764. Joseph's dislike of his second wife was inexorable; he avoided all personal contact with her, even though they shared the same apartments. Three years later Josefa too succumbed to smallpox; her widower did not even attend her funeral.

Joseph successfully defeated his mother's plans for a third marriage. He made it quite clear that the continuation of the dynasty had already been secured by the numerous sons sired by his brother Leopold in Florence.

Although the end of the Seven Years' War resulted in the loss of Silesia to Frederick II, it also secured the latter's vote at the election of the crown prince as Roman-German king. Joseph was crowned in Frankfurt in 1764, and one year later followed his father as Roman-German emperor after the latter's sudden death at Innsbruck.

Simultaneously he became co-ruler with his mother of the Habsburg crown lands. This co-regency often gave rise to sometimes serious dissensions between mother and son, caused not only by their wholly different characters but also by the usual intergenerational conflict and the associated differences of opinion.

Not until after the death of Maria Theresa in 1780 was Joseph able to introduce unopposed the reforms he had been working on for many years and which were influenced by the ideas of utilitarianism. However, his wide-ranging programme of reforms did not result in the success he had hoped for. Criticism grew, and Joseph reacted with increasing mistrust towards those around him. Lonely and isolated, he died in 1790 from the tuberculosis he had contracted on the campaign against the Turks.

Marie Christine (1742–1798), born on 13 May and thus sharing her birthday with her mother, was Maria Theresa's favourite daughter. She was called Marie by the family, Mimi by Maria Theresa (or Mimerl in Viennese dialect), and

Madame Mimi by Franz Stephan. She grew into a young girl with a graceful appearance, indulged by her mother and showered with attention by her father. This preferential treatment made her siblings very envious and led to her being excluded by them. Marie was attractive, witty, clever and talented, but also self-willed and occasionally malicious towards her siblings. She could not be trusted with any secrets without betraying them to her mother, and she treated her siblings and servants alike with complacency and haughtiness. The more favouritism shown by their mother to Marie

Marie Christine, self-portrait in a white gown. Gouache by Marie Christine, c. 1765

Marie Christine. Oil painting by the Master of the Archduchess Portraits, c. 1762/65

Christine, the more severely her siblings condemned the special position accorded their sister.

Marie Christine was the most artistically gifted member of the family and in 1776 she was even elected a member of the prestigious San Luca Academy of Arts in Rome. She painted numerous portraits of various members of the family as well as the famous genre scenes depicting the domestic bliss of the imperial family as a bourgeois idyll. The latter are copies of Dutch models, transposed into the sphere of the family. The scene depicting the distribution of gifts at the Feast of St Nicholas (6 December) shows the imperial couple with the artist surrounded by the three youngest children, Ferdinand, Maria Antonia and Maximilian Franz, who are receiving their presents. The picture was probably painted at the end of the 1750s. Dating from around 1762, the painting entitled

Childbed shows Crown Prince Joseph at the bedside of his adored wife Isabella, while the newborn infant is being fed.

A special relationship developed between Marie Christine and the beautiful, sensitive and equally gifted Isabella of Parma. The correspondence between the two young princesses, of which the half addressed to Marie Christine has been preserved, would seem to indicate that they had a passionate love affair that was hushed up by the court.

Marie Christine was the only one of Maria Theresa's children who was allowed to marry for love. With her mother's help she was able to marry Albert of Saxony-Teschen, the *"pauvre cadet"* as he called himself, who possessed neither fortune nor power. He was later to found the collection of drawings and prints at the Albertina in Vienna.

Joseph at the bed of his wife, Isabella, after the birth of their child. Gouache signed and dated by Marie Christine, 1762

Distributing the gifts in the imperial family on the Feast of St Nicholas. Gouache signed and dated by Marie Christine, 1762

Albert of Saxony-Teschen. Oil painting after J. E. Liotard, attributed to Marie Christine, c. 1767/70

In 1765 Maria Theresa appointed Albert governor of Hungary, where he resided at Pressburg. The wedding took place at Schloss Hof in the following year. After the death of Maria Theresa, Marie Christine also became the object of Joseph II's disfavour. In 1781 the childless couple were sent as governors general to the Austrian Netherlands, from where they fled in 1791 during the Revolution of Brabant, finally returning to Vienna in 1794, where Marie Christine died in 1798. To commemorate his wife Albert commissioned the famous tomb by Antonio Canova in the Church of the Augustine Friars in Vienna, and from them on lived a secluded life until his death in 1822.

Maria Elisabeth (1743–1808), the imperial couple's sixth child, was striking even as a child and grew to be an especially beautiful young woman, albeit flighty and with no special interests, according to her critical mother. Although intelligent, she tended to be superficial, enjoying gossip and bons mots, and her various governesses constantly had to encourage her to pay greater attention and apply herself to her lessons. She was not held in great affection by her siblings. Her youthful beauty made her a highly desirable match, giving rise to ambitious schemes. However, these were put paid to by a smallpox epidemic in 1767. The archduchess's pretty face was left badly disfigured by the disease, destroying all her chances on the marriage market. Later on, she also developed a goitre, which earned her the family nickname of *"kropferte Liesl"* (Puff-necked Lizzy). To the great regret of her siblings, she mourned her ravaged beauty to the end of her life. After the death of Maria Theresa the unmarried archduchess had to leave the court at Vienna like her sister Maria Anna, as Joseph II was determined not to tolerate the "petticoat rule" of his sisters any longer. Maria Elisabeth left Vienna in 1781, moving to Innsbruck where she became an abbess. She was increasingly feared for her sharp tongue, not mincing her words when putting members of the imperial family in their place. She called her nephew, the future Emperor Franz II (I), "a lout", and his brother Rainer "an ox".

Maria Elisabeth. Oil painting by the Master of the Arch-duchess Portraits, c. 1762/65

Karl Joseph (1745–1761), the second-eldest son of the imperial couple, was regarded as being especially gifted. Kind, charming and intelligent, he was not only the favourite son of Maria Theresa but equally popular within the family and at court. This popularity led to great rivalry between him and his elder brother Joseph, who was his complete opposite, being serious, reserved and difficult by nature. Karl Joseph's equable temperament promised great hopes for his future. Maria Theresa intended him to become ruler of the Grand Duchy of Tuscany and to marry him to the Bourbon princess Maria Ludovica of Spain.

When he died unexpectedly of an acute fever at the age of sixteen, his parents' hopes were destroyed. For the empress, his death ushered in a difficult period marked by disease and death.

Maria Amalia (1746–1804) was described as haughty, conceited and vivacious by her mother, who recorded the characteristics of her children, commenting on them in numerous letters. These character traits were probably fostered by the circumstance that although Maria Amalie was the eighth of sixteen children, she was brought up as an only child, just like her brother Joseph. In Joseph's case, this was occasioned by his position as crown prince, in hers by the difference in age to her elder sisters Marie Christine and Maria Elisabeth and her much younger sisters Johanna Gabriela and Maria Josefa, which precluded her being brought up and educated with them. Maria Amalia was intelligent but tended to brood, being reserved and obstinate. Sources record that she was particularly keen on hunting. Vivacious and self-willed, the archduchess developed a strong and independent personality.

Karl Joseph. Oil painting, attributed to Martin van Meytens, c. 1760

Maria Amalia. Oil painting by the Master of the Archduchess Portraits, c. 1762/65

politically active and causing numerous dissensions at the courts of Madrid, Versailles and Vienna. She was the only child to escape from her mother's influence, eventually breaking with her completely. Originally forbidden then encouraged by Maria Theresa, her contact with those of her siblings who had married Italian partners – Leopold, Marie Caroline and Ferdinand – was only sporadic, and Maria Amalie became isolated and lonely. This situation probably explains the Duchess of Parma's longing to visit Vienna, a wish that Maria Theresa strictly refused to grant her for the rest of her life.

During the course of the Napoleonic Wars, Ferdinand having died in 1802, Maria Amalie moved to Prague, where she died two years later.

She fell in love with the young and handsome Prince Karl of Zweibrücken, who was not however very wealthy. Maria Theresa, who had other plans for her daughter, rejected his suit and in 1769, aged 23, Marie Amalia was forced to marry Duke Ferdinand of Bourbon-Parma, who was five years her junior.

When Amalie was informed by her mother of the planned marriage to the duke she reacted with screaming fits and defiant behaviour. She had fervently hoped that Maria Theresa would let her choose her own husband, as the empress had done with her elder sister, Marie Christine. However, the empress demanded absolute obedience to her will, enjoining her daughter not to interfere in political affairs and to submit to her future husband, who was known to be bigoted and feeble-minded.

Although the marriage was unhappy, it produced four children. However, Marie Amalia disobeyed her mother's instructions, becoming

Maria Amalia and Ferdinand of Parma with their children. Gouache by Pompeio Batoni, 1776

Peter Leopold (1747–1792), mostly called Leopold in the family, was born at Schönbrunn and was given his first name at the request of his godmother, the Russian tsarina, Elizabeth Petrovna. He was brought up and educated together with his brother Karl Joseph, who was two years his senior. Both boys were intended to become rulers in Italy. They were keen students, with rapid powers of assimilation and good memories. Leopold showed little interest in military affairs, preferring natural sciences and technical subjects like his father, with whom he also shared a dislike of pomp and outward display. Through his tutors he was introduced to the ideas of the Enlightenment which were to have a considerable influence on his development as well as his actions as a ruler, both in Tuscany and later on when he became emperor.

As the third son he was destined for the principality of Modena and to marry Maria Beatrice d'Este. The death of his brother Karl Joseph hit him hard; the young archduke had lost the family member to whom he was closest, his playmate and schoolfellow. This painful loss no doubt reinforced his tendency to melancholy and taciturnity.

Leopold as a young boy. Oil painting by Martin van Meytens and studio, c. 1760

Peter Leopold and Karl Joseph as young boys. Oil painting by Martin van Meytens, c. 1760

Peter Leopold as Grand Duke of Tuscany. Copperplate engraving. Anonymous, c. 1765

The death of Karl Joseph also altered Maria Theresa's marriage plans. Leopold was now intended to become ruler of the Grand Duchy of Tuscany and to marry the Spanish infanta Maria Ludovica of Bourbon. During the wedding celebrations at Innsbruck in 1765 Franz Stephan died unexpectedly, and the young couple had to begin their reign in Florence immediately.

Despite the painful loss of her husband Maria Theresa felt obliged to supply her son Leopold with countless pieces of advice and instructions about his tasks as ruler. Leopold was no doubt glad to be escaping from the tutelage of his overbearing mother and the despotic behaviour of his elder brother Joseph.

He was determined to bring root and branch change to Tuscany, transforming it into a model country of the European Enlightenment. Despite his energetic will to reform, the young grand duke went about this carefully and at a moderate pace. As a far-sighted reformist politician, "Pietro Leopoldo" was very successful and enduringly popular in Italy.

Ludovica, wife of Leopold II, as bride and future grand duchess. Copperplate engraving. Anonymous, c. 1765

Grand Duke Leopold of Tuscany with his family. Gouache, anonymous after Johann Zoffany. After 1776

Following the death of his brother Joseph II in 1790, he had to leave Tuscany and assume the reins of power as Emperor Leopold II in Vienna. There he was soon confronted with the serious problems brought about by the over-hasty reforms that had been introduced by Joseph. However, Leopold had been unable to resolve these problems by the time he died suddenly only two years later.

Leopold and his wife Maria Ludovica had a model marriage and produced sixteen children within the space of twenty years, of whom only two died in childhood, thus ensuring a wealth of descendants for the imperial succession. This gave rise to the mocking remark made by Joseph describing his brother as an "outstanding populator". Nevertheless, Joseph was glad that the continuation of the dynasty had been secured by his brother.

Having refused to provide further descendants himself, Joseph II summoned Leopold's third child, Franz, to the court at Vienna in order to prepare him for his role as heir to the throne.

Leopold and Maria Ludovica with their children visiting the widowed empress. Gouache by Antonio Bencini, 1768

The relationship between the two brothers was always fraught with conflict. Joseph frequently made fun of Leopold, but nonetheless regarded him as his most intimate confidant, despite their numerous differences of opinion. The two brothers met frequently and Joseph enjoyed his visits to the grand-ducal court in Florence. They also met several times in Vienna and corresponded regularly with one another.

Ludovica with her three eldest children, including the future Emperor Franz II (I), pointing to a bust of Maria Theresa. Oil painting by Anton von Maron, c. 1770. Part of the furnishings of the Vieux-Laque Room at Schönbrunn Palace

Following a visit to Vienna in 1778/79 Leopold composed a document in code entitled *"Stato della famiglia"* in which he gave vent to his bitterness about the Viennese court and his disappointment in the family, including the constant differences with Joseph and his preferential treatment.

Emperor Joseph II and Leopold, Grand Duke of Tuscany, in Rome. Copperplate engraving by Carl Pechwell after Pompeio Batoni, c. 1770

Leopold II with his family. Etching. Anonymous, c. 1790

Ludovica, wife of Leopold II. Copperplate engraving by I. Grassy after Jacob Adam, 1791

Leopold II as Roman-German emperor. Copperplate engraving by I. Kreuzinger after Jacob Adam, 1790

Maria Carolina (1748)

Johanna Gabriela (1750–1762) and **Maria Josepha** (1751–1767) were brought up together and suffered a similar fate, both dying at a young age of smallpox. The two archduchesses were close playmates and shared the same *aia* and tutors. Maria Theresa gave stricter and more detailed instructions than in the case of her older children, covering the subjects of daily routine, hygiene and etiquette among many other topics. The two girls developed satisfactorily, worked hard at their lessons and were involved in numerous festivities in which they participated enthusiastically. When Johanna Gabriela died of smallpox in December 1762,

Johanna Gabriela and Maria Josepha. Oil painting by Pierre Benevaux, c. 1759

Maria Josepha. Oil painting by the Master of the Archduchess Portraits, c. 1765/67

her younger sister Maria Josepha was badly affected.

It was intended that Maria Josepha should marry Ferdinand IV, the Bourbon king of Naples and Sicily, for political reasons. Maria Theresa was prepared to sacrifice her daughter: "I regard poor Josepha as a victim of politics. If she only fulfils her duty towards God and her husband, and works for the salvation of her soul, then I shall be satisfied, even if she were to be unhappy". Only a few days before the wedding the young archduchess died of smallpox, and the next available sister, Maria Caroline, was married to the Neapolitan king in her stead. Josepha was deeply mourned by the family, especially by Joseph II, whose favourite sister she had been. On her deathbed she comforted her desperate mother with the words: "I would in any case have had to take my leave of you on the morrow and depart for ever. Instead I am going to heaven, where I shall be in far better keeping".

Maria Josepha. Oil painting by Martin van Meytens and studio, c. 1757/58

Maria Caroline with archducal coronet and ermine cape. Oil painting by Martin van Meytens and studio, c. 1757/58

Maria Caroline. Oil painting by the Master of the Archduchess Portraits, c. 1765/67

Maria Caroline (1752–1814), the thirteenth child in the family, was closest in character to her mother: energetic and strong-willed, frank and courageous, with an unbridled temperament and a strong instinct for independence. She was called Charlotte by the family and brought up together with her younger sister, Maria Antonia, causing no little trouble to her *aia*. At the age of fifteen she even had the courage to beg her mother to change her tutors; to everybody's surprise, Maria Theresa agreed, but wrote her a letter containing both reproof and praise as well as exhorting her to apply herself to her lessons from then on. With the death of her sister Maria Josepha, Maria Caroline's life changed decisively. In 1768 she had to take her late sister's place and marry Ferdinand IV, son of the Spanish king Charles III, who had ascended the throne of Naples in 1767, just after his sixteenth birthday. Equipped by her mother with a memorandum dealing with etiquette in private and political affairs, the young archduchess travelled south to meet her fate. Energetic and enterprising like her mother, she soon had the upper hand over her wholly unmannerly and unattractive spouse, who was popularly called *il re nasone* on account of his long nose. He was uncouth (earning him another nickname, *il re lazzarone* or knavish king), indolent and interested more in hunting and other pleasures than the business of ruling.

King Ferdinand of Naples and Sicily with Maria Caroline and their children. Gouache by Carlo Marsigli, 1775

Only a few months after her arrival in Naples Maria Caroline wrote to her former *aia* describing the wedding night for which, like her sisters, she had been only inadequately prepared: "I freely admit that I would rather die than have to go through all that again … I now know what marriage is, and feel the deepest sympathy for Maria Antonia, who has yet to marry".

Maria Caroline succeeded in prevailing against her husband. She bore seventeen children (of whom only four outlived their mother), and subsequently pursued a similar form of marriage policy to her mother at the Viennese court.

She married her eldest daughter, Maria Theresa, to her nephew Franz, Leopold's eldest son, who succeeded his father as Emperor Franz II. The young queen succeeded in gradually assuming the reins of government herself, introducing a comprehensive programme of reforms. She was also instrumental in founding

Monument to Queen Maria Caroline of Naples and Sicily in the gardens of Schönbrunn Palace

the Academy of Sciences in Naples. Despite her affection for her mother, she kept her at a distance and did not allow her to interfere in her political activities or private life.

Marie Caroline, who was also a protector of the Freemasons, was a decided opponent of the French Revolution and of Napoleon, from whom she and her family were forced to flee. She was outraged at the marriage of her granddaughter Marie Louise, the daughter of Franz II (I), to Napoleon Bonaparte, remarking "To crown it all I am now the Devil's grandmother".

In the latter years of her marriage she became increasingly unhappy, especially as Ferdinand began to spend ever more time pursuing extramarital affairs, leading to the couple's estrangement.

Fleeing from Napoleon she returned to her beloved Vienna, where she died during the Congress of Vienna in 1814. She had a memorial erected in the park at Schönbrunn depicting herself with four of her children in a medallion.

Ferdinand with archducal coronet and ermine cape. Oil painting by Martin van Meytens and studio, c. 1758/59

Ferdinand Karl (1754–1806), who was said to be the handsomest of Maria Theresa's sons, was also her problem child. The second youngest son, he was constantly criticised by his mother for neglecting his religious and other duties. She rebuked him for being careless, pleasure-seeking, weak-willed, idle and slovenly, as documented in her numerous letters.

Maria Theresa had already chosen a wife for this son, too, namely the daughter of the Duke of Modena, Maria Beatrice d'Este, originally intended for Karl Joseph, then for Peter Leopold. Regarded highly by Maria Theresa, she was four years older than her future husband, no beauty, but clever and level-headed. Maria

Theresa entrusted her son's fate to his bride, corresponding with her at length well before the wedding.

In 1771, at the age of seventeen, Ferdinand left the court at Vienna to reside with his wife at the court in Milan. The couple had a harmo-

Archduke Ferdinand with his sister, Maria Caroline. Oil painting by Martin van Meytens, c. 1760/62

Archduke Ferdinand and Beatrice d'Este with their children. Gouache by Gaetano Perego, 1776

nious marriage; Ferdinand, who tended towards laziness, devoted himself to his interest in the fine arts and to his other predilections. Maria Beatrice, who far surpassed him in shrewdness and intelligence, devoted herself to the family and the upbringing of their children. The latter did not start to appear for some time, a circumstance which prompted a barrage of advice from the empress in Vienna. Neither did she neglect to take her son to task, prescribing his duties in letter after letter.

In her letters, Maria Theresa also constantly expressed her desire for grandchildren, demanding them as her due right for her own pleasure. Maria Beatrice bore a total of nine children. The couple's youngest child, Maria Ludovica, was to become the second wife of Ferdinand's nephew, Emperor Franz II (I).

The grandchildren's upbringing was overseen and directed by their grandmother in Vienna, who was constantly worried about their development and health. Remarkably, Maria Theresa never met the grandchildren who did not live in Vienna; she knew the children solely from the portraits she commissioned of them, using these as a basis for her observations and characterisations.

Fleeing before Napoleon's army, the archducal family had to leave Milan in 1796, eventually ending up in Vienna. Ferdinand died in 1802; his wife, from 1808 the mother-in-law of the emperor, survived her husband by twenty-three years.

The youngest daughter, **Maria Antonia** (1755–1793), was an exceptionally pretty and graceful child; spoilt and loved by all the family, she was herself especially fond of her eldest brother, Joseph, to whom she remained closest for the rest of her life. She was intended to realise her mother's most ambitious marriage plans. While she was still a very small child, negotiations were initiated between Vienna and Versailles on a possible marriage to the French dauphin, the future Louis XVI. Maria Antonia's education was intended to prepare her for her future role as Queen of France. Frequently criticised by her mother for her flightiness and love of pleasure, Maria Antonia was taught French language and literature, with special emphasis on music, singing, dancing, drawing and handiwork.

Vivacious and high-spirited, the archduchess was quick to grasp a subject but was generally inattentive and fonder of play than learning. She also showed little inclination to apply herself to a subject seriously. When the plans for her marriage became concrete, it was obvious that she would have to undergo a concerted programme of education to close the considerable gaps in her knowledge. At the age of

Maria Antonia. Oil painting by Martin van Meytens and studio, c. 1758/59

fourteen, the archduchess was regarded as well-educated and musical, but according to sources, compared to the standards of the time she displayed "a superficial mind and an arrogant character with scant talent for diplomacy".

Maria Antonia as leading lady with her brothers Ferdinand and Maximilian in the pastoral ballet Trionfo d' Amore *by Christoph Willibald Gluck performed on the occasion of the marriage of Joseph and Josefa of Bavaria in January 1765. Oil painting by Martin van Meytens and studio. After 1765*

In 1770 Maria Antonia left the court at Vienna to take up residence as the future queen of France at Versailles, equipped with the instructions and well-meant advice on her forthcoming duties as wife and mother that Maria Theresa gave all her daughters on their marriage.

At their first encounter at Compiègne, the fifteen-year-old bridegroom appeared shy and inhibited, a short-sighted youth whom Marie Antoinette, as she was called from then on at the French court, had probably imagined quite differently. It was soon clear that the marriage with the heir to the French throne had not been consummated. At first, this was ascribed to the dauphin's shyness and inexperience. When Joseph II, Marie Antoinette's favourite brother, visited the couple at Versailles in 1777, he had a private talk with his brother-in-law in which it emerged that Louis XVI was suffering from a psychological block which prevented him from consummating the sexual act. Until recently historians had erroneously assumed that he was suffering from phimosis, a condition subsequently relieved by a minor operation. However, this is not confirmed by any sources. Evidently the enlightening talk with his brother-in-law did the trick, as Marie Antoinette wrote joyfully to her mother in Vienna that the marriage had at last been consummated, and she soon found herself pregnant. Marie Antoinette had four children, of whom only their daughter, known as "Madame Royale", survived the French Revolution.

Maria Antonia. Oil painting, attributed to Marie Christine, c. 1763/65

Marie Antoinette as dauphine in a red hunting habit. Pastel by Joseph Kranzinger, c. 1772

As queen, during a period when France was at war with Britain, Marie Antoinette was fiercely criticised for being frivolous and extravagant. Joseph II had entrusted her with the task of representing Austria's interests following the death of Maria Theresa, a position that brought her into open conflict with the French government, giving rise to the suspicion that she was trying to influence policy in favour of Habsburg hegemony in Europe. Reviled as *l' autrichienne* (the Austrian woman), she was detested by the French people. In October 1789 the French Revolution broke out: Versailles was stormed and the royal family taken to Paris,

Marie Antoinette as Queen of France. Marble bust by Joseph Fernande, 1779

where they resided at the Tuileries. In 1791 France became a constitutional monarchy, and in 1792 the National Assembly declared war on Austria. Numerous defeats at the hands of enemy armies gave new fuel to the revolutionary forces, with the Republicans demanding the overthrow of the monarchy. The royal family suffered a cruelly harsh fate: captured while attempting to flee France, Louis XVI was put on trial, condemned and executed in January 1793; following a show trial Marie Antoinette was taken to the guillotine and beheaded in October of the same year.

Marie Antoinette, King Louis XVI of France and Archduke Maximilian. Oil painting by Joseph Hauzinger, 1778

The youngest son **Maximilian** (1756–1801), called Max Franz by the family, developed satisfactorily under the supervision of his trusted tutors – he was well-built, hardy and truth-loving, with a generous, open nature, a quick mind and a good memory. According to his tutor his less attractive qualities included stubbornness, reserve and taciturnity. He was brought up and educated together with his slightly older brother Ferdinand, and intro-

Archduke Maximilian. Oil painting by Martin van Meytens and studio, c. 1760

duced to Enlightenment thinking, which was to have an enduring influence on him. His mother decided that he would not be suited to marriage and in 1774 sent him on the "Cavaliers' Tour", a kind of Grand Tour for the scions of noble families which took the young archduke to the courts of his married sisters in Italy and Versailles. Like all his siblings, before he embarked on his travels, he was given written rules of conduct and maxims for life by his mother.

Maria Theresa had agreed with Joseph II that he should embark on a military career on his return to Vienna. This was a prerequisite for the governorship of Hungary, a position that she had reserved for her son. To general surprise the rather phlegmatic archduke demonstrated pronounced military gifts, but his career in the army was abruptly terminated when he fell seriously ill during the War of the Bavarian Succession. Mother and brother decided that the young archduke should now pursue a career in the Church with political influence as prince-elector of Cologne and archbishop of Münster. After the opposition of the German prince-electors had been successfully overcome, his position as the next prince-elector of Cologne was secure. In 1780 he also succeeded to the title of Grand Master of the Teutonic Knights which passed to him on the death of his uncle, Charles of Lorraine. The ecclesiastical career planned for him by his mother as the most suitable path for the future maintenance of "an eighth archduke", as Maria Theresa noted in her instructions, was secured and in 1784, following the death of the previous elector, he took up his official duties in Cologne and Münster.

Maximilian had thus assumed the rank of a sovereign ecclesiastical ruler, and like his brother Leopold, began to institute a programme of moderate reform.

Plagued by narcolepsy and coughing fits, Max Franz became depressed and so corpulent that he was almost immobile by the age of forty. He too was forced to flee from Napoleon's army, returning to Vienna in 1800, where a year later he died of a stroke following a sumptuous meal.

Art at the court of Maria Theresa

On ascending the throne, Maria Theresa was fully occupied in defending her heritage, which meant drawing on financial reserves that were in any case hardly abundant. She thus had little time or money to concern herself with art for art's sake, and her practical nature would probably have regarded this as a waste of money and time that could have better been devoted to work. Nonetheless, Maria Theresa appreciated the important role that architecture, art and craftsmanship had to play in representing the pomp and magnificence of the court.

European palatial architecture was generally influenced by French models. The predominant taste at the court of Louis XIV was one of refined and sumptuous opulence, setting the tone and constituting a model for the display of rank and pomp at princely courts. Despite this basic dependence on the French model, the Viennese court was very different to the court at Versailles; in the eyes of the strait-laced and deeply Catholic Maria Theresa, the latter was profligate almost to the point of indecency. In comparison to France, the Habsburg residences were all but modest; rather than a constant programme of new construction, old complexes such as the Vienna Hofburg were converted, extended and modernised.

Prospectus Propilei Principalis Palatij Cæsarei versus forum carboniorum secundum factam modellam perficiendi .   *Prospect der Haupt Facciade von der Kays: Burg, wie solche gegen dem Kohl - Marckt solte zusehen kommen, nach dem daselbst befindenden Modell gezeichnet .*

View of the main façade of the imperial palace. Copperplate engraving by Salomon Kleiner, 1733

Schönbrunn Palace, façade facing the cour d'honneur

In terms of her personal tastes, like many other monarchs, Maria Theresa had a predilection for commissioning architectural projects. She followed with great interest and dedication the most important building project of her reign, the transformation of the hunting lodge at Schönbrunn into an imperial residence, on which work began in 1743. Nikolaus Pacassi emerged as the architect most congenial to the empress's tastes and eventually became responsible for almost all the building projects initiated by the empress. He understood how to accommodate the concrete and practical wishes of his patron while uniting early neo-Classical forms with opulent Rococo ornamentation. Pacassi also modernised the other Habsburg residences at Pressburg, Budapest, Prague and Innsbruck.

The Great Gallery at Schönbrunn Palace

Even later on in her reign, Maria Theresa did not commission any new building projects for her own use. She purchased palatial seats and had them adapted, for example the magnificent complex of the Belvedere in Vienna, acquired from the heirs of Prince Eugene of Savoy, or Schloss Hof, located forty kilometres from Vienna on the River March, that was famed throughout Europe for its Baroque gardens.

For the interiors of her residences Maria Theresa favoured exotic elements, referred to at that time as "Indian" decoration, which included Indo-Persian miniatures, Chinese porcelain and lacquer work. Maria Theresa herself commented on this predilection of hers, noting: "I think nothing of import in the world except what comes from India; lacquer work and wall-hangings give me especial pleasure".

The Round Chinese Cabinet at Schönbrunn Palace

Paintings constituted an important decorative element in the interiors of her palaces, and here Maria Theresa's tastes were above all for portraits and scenes documenting the numerous ceremonies and family celebrations. Her favourite court artist for these commissions was Martin van Meytens, who specialised not only in portraiture but also in these mostly large-scale paintings which he accomplished with the aid of the numerous assistants working in his studio. His work is characterised by its combination of observation and attention to detail together with a virtuoso rendering of material surfaces. His group paintings, for example the cycle depicting the marriage of Joseph II to Isabella of Parma, or the coronation at Frankfurt, are accretive in their composition and purely documentary in tone, without any attempt at the heroisation or foregrounding of any particular person.

Maria Theresa's favourite artist was the Genevan painter Jean-Étienne Liotard, with whom she enjoyed a truly amicable relationship that endured over several decades. Specialising in pastels, Liotard arrived in Vienna in 1743 on his return journey from Istanbul where he had spent several years. With his Turkish dress and long beard, he caused a sensation, and his exotic appearance also gained him entry to the court. He subsequently made several visits to Vienna, painting numerous portraits of Maria Theresa, her husband and their children. The empress had a predilection for pastel painting and purchased countless examples of work that the artist brought with him and which never failed to appeal to her.

From her childhood onwards, Maria Theresa had attended theatrical performances during family celebrations at court, not only as a spectator but also as a singer and dancer. Music had been cultivated at the Viennese court since the 17th century, and several members of the imperial family had demonstrated considerable talent in this field, including Emperor Leopold I, who composed works that surpass by far

Mlle. Suzanne Curchod, later Mme. Necker, wife of the French minister of finance.
Pastel by Jean Étienne Liotard, c. 1760

The Millions Room at Schönbrunn Palace

the usual levels of princely dilettantism. Music also flourished at the court of Maria Theresa, with composers who are today still famous all over the world, including Wolfgang Amadeus Mozart, who performed for the empress at Schönbrunn as a six-year-old, Joseph Haydn and Christoph Willibald Gluck.

Girl with doll. Pastel by Jean Étienne Liotard, c. 1760

Bibliography

Etzelsdorfer, Hannes. *Maria Theresia. Kinder, Kirche, Korsett.* 2009

Hamann, Brigitte. *Die Habsburger. Biographisches Lexikon.* Reissued 2001

Koschatzky, Walter (ed.). *Maria Theresia und ihre Zeit.* 1980

Maria Theresia und ihre Zeit. Zur 200. Wiederkehr des Todestages. Exhibition catalogue 1980

Mraz, Gerda and Gottfried. *Maria Theresia. Ihr Leben und ihre Zeit in Bildern und Dokumenten.* 1980

Weissensteiner, Friedrich. *Die Töchter Maria Theresias.* 1994

Weissensteiner, Friedrich. *Die Söhne Maria Theresias.* 2004

Weiss, Sabine. *Zur Herrschaft geboren. Kindheit und Jugend im Haus Habsburg von Kaiser Maximilian bis Kronprinz Rudolf.* 2008

Zedinger, Renate (ed.). *Lothringens Erbe. Franz Stephan von Lothringen (1708–1765) und sein Wirken in Wirtschaft, Wissenschaft und Kunst der Habsburgermonarchie.* Exhibition catalogue. 2000

Picture credits

**Schloß Schönbrunn
Kultur- und Betriebsges.m.b.H.**
Cover, 4/4, 14 (SR), 15 (JW), 16 (EK), 18 (SR), 21 (EK), 23 above (EK), 23 below (EK), 24 above (SR), 24 below (SR), 25 above (EK), 25 below (SR), 26 (SR), 27 (SR), 28 (EK), 30 (FS), 32 r. (FS), 32 l. (MK), 33 above (MK), 33 below (MK), 34 (EK), 35 (SR), 36 (AK), 37 below (MK), 38 above (EK), 38 below (SR), 39 above (SR), 39 below (EK), 40 (EK), 41 (EK), 42 (EK), 43 (EK), 44 above (SR), 45 (SR), 46 below (EK), 47 above (EK), 47 below (SR), 51 r. (EK), 52 above (JW), 52 below (JH), 54 above (SR), 54 below (EK), 55 (EK), 56 above (EK), 56 below l. (SR), 56 below r. (SR), 62 (AK), 63 below (EK), 67 above (SR), 67 below (EK), 68 above (EK), 71 (SW), 72 above (AK), 72 below (AK), 73 (AK), 74 (EK), 75 above (AK), 75 below (EK)

Kunsthistorisches Museum/Schloß Schönbrunn
8 below, 11 below, 12 (EK), 29, 31, 37 above, 44 below, 46 above, 48, 49 (SR), 50 above, 51 l. (SR), 57 (SR), 58 (SR), 59 (SR), 60 above (SR), 60 below, 63 above (SR), 65 (SR), 69 (SR)

Kunsthistorisches Museum/Kaiserappartements
66 (SR)

Kunsthistorisches Museum
11 above, 68 below (FS)

Nationalbank/Schloß Schönbrunn
19 (EK)

Bundesmobilienverwaltung
8 above (MH), 10 above (TK), 22 (SM), 50 below (MH), 53 (MH), 61 (TK), 64 (TK)

Private collection
10 below (FS)

Photography:
Marianne Haller (MH)
Tina King (TK)
Markus Klasz (MK)
Edgar Knaack (EK)
Alexander Koller (AK)
Sascha Rieger (SR)
Franz Schachinger (FS)
Fritz Simak (FS)
Studio Milar (SM)
Johannes Wagner (JW)